Flawed

Hope for Men

Study Guide

ROLLAND KENNESON

www.2t22.org

Paper back ISBN-13: 978-1-946469-75-5

ShelteringTree.Earth, LLC Publishing
PO Box 973, Eagle Lake, FL 33839

Did you enjoy this book?

We love to hear from our readers.

Please visit the author at
ShelteringTreeMedia.com

About the Cover:
The main photo is by Earl Wilcox and provided through Unsplash.com/license.

CONTENTS

ROLLAND KENNESON

Getting the Most Out of This Study

Thank you for leading or participating in this 8-week study through *Flawed to Fruitful: Hope for Men*. I pray that the time you put into reading the book, the work you will do through this study guide, and the discussion you will have in your small group will build you up in your faith in our Lord Jesus Christ. Here are some helpful hints for those leading the study.

1. Each person needs to come prepared by bringing a Bible, a copy of *Flawed to Fruitful: Hope for Men*, and copy of this study guide to each session. (For discount copies, see the publisher's shop https://www.shelteringtreemedia.com/shop/ministry)

2. Make sure to clearly communicate the group guidelines before any discussion starts. These guidelines would include issues as group confidentiality, using only words that build up, commitment to honesty, commitment to do each session's reading and workbook, expectation of participation in discussion, etc. Once these guidelines are set, act as the guardian of the discussion so the group functions within these guidelines.

3. Copies of the book and study guide can be handed out during the first session. This study was intentionally designed so no reading or work are absolutely required before the first session.

However, participants could answer Session 1 questions beforehand to be more prepared for the discussion. Reading through the chapters of the book begins in Session 2. This will allow you to take time in the first session to get acquainted, set up group guidelines, and discuss expectations of the study.

4. There are seven to nine questions each week. Each participant should read the appropriate chapter and write out their answers for each session's questions before meeting with the group. During each session, the leader should simply ask participants how they answered the questions and lead a discussion based on what the participants share. Feel free to add in related questions since you know best what your group needs. However, when you ask a question, remember to be comfortable with silence. If you ask, "Would someone share how you responded to the question, *How is lust an idol?*", be patience and wait for someone to answer. *Silence is OK; it means the men are thinking, processing, and maybe even gaining courage to speak. Do not take that away from them by speaking too quickly after asking a question. If no one responds, ask the question again or rephrase the question.*

5. The final session of the study was intentionally built to help each man move into becoming a disciple-maker. One of the best ways for a man to be spiritually fruitful is to invest in the next generation. Therefore, Session 8 consists of a list of accountability questions as well as an exercise of praying and seeking out a mentor

as well as a protégé. Since each man should have completed the book and the study guide, then each man should be ready to lead another man through both. Do not be tempted to skip this last session. Challenge each man to think, pray, and seek out someone in which they could invest their life.

6. Remember that you are not teaching *a lesson,* but rather, you are leading men to discuss what is important to them. Do not rush through discussion in order to cover all the questions in the session. If you do not get to all the questions in the session, but the men are having relevant dialogue during your time together, that is a success.

SESSION 1

Recognizing the Truth About Our Flaws

1. Have you ever created something with your own hands? Tell about your very first attempt at it. How did it turn out?

2. How did you feel when you found a mistake or a flaw in your work? How long did it take you to master this work?

3. Read Jeremiah 18:1-5. How do you think God felt when His people, the work of His hands, proudly displayed their spiritual flaws?

4. Read John 17:3, 1 John 5:11-13, and John 3:16. Can you recall a moment in your life when you turned away from your sin, surrendered your life to Jesus, and was born again? Briefly share how that happened.

5. How do you feel when your spiritual flaws unexpectedly rear their ugly heads?

6. Read Exodus 34:6, Psalm 145:8-9, and 1 John 1:9-10. In light of these verses, and many more like them, how do you believe God feels about the spiritual flaws in your life?

7. Read Romans 8:1, Ephesians 1:7 and Hebrews 8:12. In light of these verses, how should you feel when your spiritual flaws are on display in your life?

8. This study will examine anger, fear, lust, depression, and inconsistency. Which one of these issues do you struggle with the most? Explain your answer.

9. Read Romans 6:1-7, Hebrews 12:1-5, and 1 John 3:4-10. How do these verses provide you with hope for conquering these issues?

Hope for Men

So, the spiritual traps covered in this book do not have to ensnare us. When we struggle with them, Jesus can transform us into His likeness. He can take a flawed piece of clay and reshape it into what He desires. He can take a flawed man and make him fruitful again. This is my prayer for you. (pg. 3)

Prayer

Heavenly Father, as I begin this study, I ask that You reveal in me any flaw You want to correct. Help me surrender to You as a piece of clay in the potter's hands. Transform me into Your likeness and make me fruitful for Your Kingdom and glory. In Jesus' name I pray. Amen.

Memory Verse

Then the LORD passed by in front of him and proclaimed, "The LORD, the LORD God, compassionate and gracious, slow to anger, and abounding in lovingkindness and truth; who keeps lovingkindness for thousands, who forgives iniquity, transgression and sin. (Exodus 34:6-7a)

SESSION 2

Flawed by Anger; Fruitful by God's Grace

Introduction and Chapter 1
Pages 1-31

1. Have you ever ignored the *check engine* light in your vehicle? For how long? What happened when you ignored it for too long?

2. In what ways is anger like our spiritual *check engine* light?

3. On a scale from 1 to 10, with 1 being "Never" and 10 being "All the time," how often does anger play a part in your life?

4. Some of Moses' anger triggers were *change, loss, crisis, and criticism*. Do any of these turn on the *check engine* light of anger for you? Can you share a time when that happened?

5. Think back to the last time you were angry and ask yourself, "Why was I angry?" Were you afraid, frustrated, confused, or hurt? Why? (Answering these questions will help you get to the root of your anger).

6. Read Numbers 20:6-8 and pages 17-21. From these passages, what can we learn about how to correctly respond to anger? Which of the five correct responses help you the most when you are angry? Why?

7. Read Numbers 27:14 and Psalm 106:32-33 (preferably in the NIV, ESV, or CSB). In speaking about Moses' anger at this event, what do these verses teach us about the danger of our anger?

8. Read Numbers 20:11-13 and pages 27-30. What consequences did Moses suffer because of his anger? Which of these do you relate to most? Explain.

9.   *Think about how our temper could be diffused if we simply step away from the situation and turn toward God. We know where we will meet God: in His Word. When we get on our knees before the Lord with the Scripture and prayerfully seek resolution of a tense situation, we will find our Father giving us wise and good instruction. This is the correct way to respond when anger begins to rear its ugly head.* (pg. 21)

How have you seen this response to anger prevent negative consequences?

What is one aspect of this passage you could implement this week to relieve the prospect of anger in your life?

Hope for Men

If you struggle with anger, spend some time praying about the root of this anger. Examine the circumstances when that anger flares up. What is going on when you are angry and how is that manifested in your life? Ask the questions "Why am I angry? Am I hurt, frustrated, confused, or fearful?" When you identify why the check engine light has come on, ask yourself, "Why did this hurt me, or frustrate me, or confuse me, or scare me?" This examination will help you allow the Spirit of God work in your life to remove that anger. (pg. 31)

Prayer

Holy God, I confess my struggle with anger. Please show me the root of this anger and then please work in my life to cut out that root. When my anger begins to flare up, teach me to step away from the situation and step toward You. Let Your peace reign in my emotions. In the powerful name of Jesus. Amen.

Memory Verse

Then Moses and Aaron came in from the presence of the assembly to the doorway of the tent of meeting and fell on their faces. Then the glory of the LORD appeared to them. (Numbers 20:6)

SESSION 3

Flawed by Fear; Fruitful by God's Spirit

Chapter 2
Pages 33-68

1. When was the last time you were really afraid? What caused that fear? Was it a *fun* scare (like a scary movie or a haunted house) or was it a *real* fear (like the possibility of losing someone or a dire diagnosis)?

2. On a scale from 1 to 10, with 1 being "Never" and 10 being "Always," how often does fear play a part in your spiritual life?

3. Gideon's story teaches us that fear causes us to question God's goodness, His faithfulness, His view of us, and His Word. Have you ever seen this exemplified in your life? If so, which one of these responses is more common for you?

4.   *Fear fights against our faith and keeps us stunted spiritually.*   (pg. 45)

Do you agree with this? Why or why not?

5. How have you seen God's power and presence melt your fear and anxiety away? Briefly share what happened.

6. Read Judges 6:34, 1 Chronicles 12:18, and 2 Chronicles 24:20 and pages 58-59 (especially the footnote on page 58). What role does the Holy Spirit play in removing our fear? What happens when the Holy Spirit *comes upon* someone who might be gripped by fear?

7.   *Arrogance in a man's life can be a way for him to hide the fear that lies deeper inside him. There is a close relationship between fear and arrogance. There are some who define arrogance as the fear of transparency. It starts as a fear that someone will see who I really am, they will judge me for it, and I will be found wanting. Eventually, that fear manifests itself as arrogance.* (pg. 65)

Have you ever seen the relationship between fear and arrogance in your life or in another's life? Share that experience noting how the arrogance was a mask for fear.

8. Do you have a trusted man in your life, or a group of reliable, faithful men with whom you can be transparent about your fears, as well as other spiritual issues? If so, contact them and talk with them about what you worked through in this session. If not, spend some time praying and identifying someone to fulfill that role in your life.

Hope for Men

This is exactly what our Heavenly Father does for us when we face our own fears. We call out in fear, and He comes running. We see this in Gideon's life. When he needed God, the Holy Spirit fell upon him to accomplish the task God required of him. We see it in our life when we call out to God and He responds to us in grace and love. (pg. 63)

Prayer

Almighty Father, there are times when my fear has a battle with my faith. I have tried to hide it from others, but I cannot hide it from You. Fear has stunted me spiritually so I pray You will remove that fear from me. I ask that Your Spirit take control of me and make the valiant warrior You have created me to be. Thank You for Your power and presence. Amen.

Memory Verse

The angel of the LORD appeared to him and said to him, "The LORD is with you, O valiant warrior." (Judges 6:12)

SESSION 4

Flawed by Lust; Fruitful by God's Mercy

Chapter 3
Pages 69-90

1. Why does is seem that lust is more of a problem with men than with women? Is lust just a *young man's* sin?

2. On a scale from 1 to 10, with 1 being "Rarely" and 10 being "Constantly," how often does lust hinder your spiritual life?

3. *There are really only two types of men: Those who struggle with lust, and those who lie.* (pg. 72)

   What does that mean? Do you agree? Why or why not?

4. How is lust a form of idolatry?

5. If a culture of lust in your inner life is created by allowing sensuality a place in your life, becoming complacent, and being indulgent (pg. 74-77), then which of these plays the major role in your life? What steps can you take today to find victory in this area?

6. Have you ever been caught living in your personal culture of lust? How did trying to hide it work for you? Can you ever hide it from God?

7. Why is it natural for men to attempt to hide lustful
    behavior? David resorted to murder to hide this sin. While
    we have probably not resorted to such drastic measures,
    what lengths have you gone to in order to hide your lust?

8.   *You can't hide your sin. It will manifest in your life
    somehow. In previous chapters we have examined anger,
    fear, and arrogance. There is a real possibility that these
    are in your life because you are hiding the sin of lust. You
    may believe you are hiding your pornography addiction
    and think there is no collateral damage. But sin never hurts
    only you. It is freeing to unburden yourself from that sin by
    sharing it with others – your spouse, your mentor, your
    brothers in the Lord. It will provide you accountability and
    a chance to be honest and open about your sin.* (pg. 85)

    Who do you know well enough to share this part of your
    life in order to be free from the secret shame and guilt of
    lust? Contact them today and share your heart with them.

9. If you have been freed from the grip of lust in your life, share how God showed you mercy. Did He send you a friend or confidant who helped you? What role did confession play? How can you help other men find this same victory?

Hope for Men

Here is the good news! God gives us mercy! God does not give us what we deserve! He provides forgiveness, freedom, and hope! Lust in our lives needs to be removed and God can remove it, forgive us, and restore us. (pg. 86)

Prayer

My Great Creator and Redeemer, I need Your mercy today. I am so tired of being controlled by my lust and I cry out to You to free me from these chains! Thank you that in Jesus Christ, we do not receive what we deserve but instead You provide us forgiveness. Give me the spiritual, emotional, and moral strength to remove lust from my life and become the man You want me to be. Amen.

Memory Verse

Now flee from youthful lusts and pursue righteousness, faith, love and peace, with those who call on the Lord from a pure heart. (2 Timothy 2:22)

SESSION 5

Flawed by Depression; Fruitful by God's Presence

Chapter 4
Pages 91-110

1. Have you ever experienced some level of temporary depression? If so, what was the instigating factor? (For example, weather, time of year, holiday season, a relationship, circumstances, a loss of some kind, etc.) *If you experience **long-term or clinical depression**, please speak to a Christian counselor or a Christian psychologist. While this chapter may bring help and encouragement, it is specifically about **temporary depression** which many men face.*

2. On a scale from 1 to 10, with 1 being "Never" and 10 being "A lot of the time," how often do you experience a spiritual funk?

3. Have you ever tried to find an answer to your temporary depression in something other than Jesus Christ? What was the outcome?

4. Has conflict or confrontation ever played a part in your depression (like being falsely accused or not being heard)? Briefly, explain the experience and tell how God's presence provided you encouragement.

5. Have threats ever played a part in your depression (like the threat of losing your job, your marriage, your health, or maybe even physical violence)? Briefly share the experience and tell how God's presence provided you encouragement.

6. Has isolation ever played a part in your depression? Briefly share the experience and tell how God's presence provided you encouragement.

7. How have you experienced the powerful escape from depression through God's loving response of simply providing you rest and nourishment? Why is a good night's sleep and a healthy meal important to maintain when depression sets in?

8. Have you ever experienced a unique display of God's power as you wrestled through your depression? If so, what effect did that have on you?

9. In what ways has the awareness of God's presence helped you stave off or have victory over your depression?

Hope for Men

Elijah had thought he was on his own: "I alone am left." He had relied on his own strength and ended up in hopelessness. God's loving response was to remind Elijah not only of His incredible power but also of His interminable presence. Elijah was never alone but God graciously provided him a physical manifestation of His presence to remind Elijah he was never alone.

One important aspect to overcome depression is understanding and becoming aware of God's power and presence in your life. (pg. 105-106)

Prayer

My Ever-present King, there are times when life seems like it is just too much for me. There are times when a sadness, a funk, a spiritual depression comes over me. God, when this happens, please give me a powerful, real sense of Your presence surrounding me. Remind me that You will never leave me nor forsake me and that You are always walking with me through this life. Thank you for Your power, Your presence, and Your love. In Jesus' name. Amen.

Memory Verse

The angel of the LORD came again a second time and touched him and said, "Arise, eat, because the journey is too great for you." (1 Kings 19:7)

SESSION 6

Flawed by Inconsistency; Fruitful by Restoration

Chapter 5
Pages 111-131

1. What are some other words that could be used for *inconsistency*?

2. On a scale from 1 to 10, with 1 being "Wishy-washy" and 10 being "Rock solid," how consistent is your walk with Jesus Christ?

3. What evidence would you give in a court that speaks to your consistent relationship with Jesus?

4. What evidence would a prosecutor provide against you in court which would speak to your inconsistency in your relationship with Jesus?

5.   *The Father Himself spoke and told Simon, "Listen to Him! Stop talking for one second so you can actually listen to Jesus!"*

    This is the key to the inconsistency in Simon Peter. When Peter was listening to Jesus, really listening to what Jesus was saying and fully grasping what His Kingdom was about, Peter was "The Rock." But when Peter expressed his own desires over the desires of Jesus, when Peter's plans overtook the plans of the Father, he slipped into his old character of Simon. (pg. 122)

How has this passage proved to be true in your spiritual life? How has listening to Jesus and His Word contributed to your spiritual consistency?

6. How does the story of Peter's restoration after his three-fold denial of Jesus bring you encouragement? Have you experienced restoration for you sins by asking Jesus into your life as Savior and Lord?

7. *Peter was his best when he was fully trusting in Christ and fully surrendered to the Holy Spirit. We must remember that it was only Peter who trusted Christ enough to get out of the boat and walk on water. It is only Peter who declared that Jesus was the Christ, the Son of the Living God, even if it was not a popular stand. It was only Peter who boldly preached on Pentecost, defied orders to stop preaching, and was even imprisoned for preaching Christ and Him crucified.* (pg. 130)

Discuss how this passage might give hope to those who struggle with spiritual inconsistency? What is the key to spiritual consistency?

Hope for Men

We can learn a lot from Peter. If a person was reading about our walk with Christ like we read about Peter's, there would times we, too, would look like a plain ol' Simon and other times we would be like Peter, "the Rock."

But like Peter, we are at our best when we are fully trusting in Christ and fully surrendered to the Holy Spirit. (pg. 130)

Prayer

Oh God, You, and You alone, are my Solid Rock. Forgive me when I have denied You, when I have inconsistently followed You, and failed to be who You called me to be. Give me courage, give me strength, and give me the desire to follow You well each and every day in the strength of Jesus. In His name I pray. Amen.

Memory Verse

I also say to you that you are Peter, and upon this rock I will build My church; and the gates of Hades will not overpower it. (Matthew 16:18)

SESSION 7

Flawed to Fruitful; Hope for Men

Chapter 6
Pages 133-154

1. How long ago did you give your life to Jesus and were saved from sin and death? Can you describe the progress of your spiritual growth since then? (rapid, slow at first, up and down, etc.)

2. Of the five topics discussed so far in this book (anger, fear, lust, depression, and inconsistency), which one is your biggest struggle?

3. Read Ephesians 4:26-27. What three commands does Paul provide for battling anger? Which one of them could you apply this week to combat anger in your life? How?

4. Read Philippians 4:6-7. What is the command regarding anxiety or fear? How does Paul suggest you battle the fear in your life? What can you do this week to improve your prayer life?

5. Read Romans 7:18-19, 24-25a, and 1 Corinthians 9:24-27. Where does Paul find the power, will, and desire to conquer his fleshly desires (Romans 7:24-25a). What actions should we take to discipline ourselves in the area of lust?

6. Read 2 Corinthains 10:3-5 and Philippians 3:13-14. What can we learn in these passages regarding thoughts of depression? How does focusing on our future life with Jesus help us work through depression?

7. Read Ephesians 6:13-17 and 1 Corinthians 15:58. How does the armor of God provide us with the strength and ability to be consistent in our spiritual life? How is abounding in the work of the Lord connected to being consistent and immovable in our spiritual life?

8. What activities or principles can you implement in your walk with Jesus that would help you remember that God uses flawed men and makes them fruitful for His Kingdom and His glory?

Hope for Men

The issues addressed throughout this book – anger, fear, lust, depression, inconsistency – do not have to be ministry-ending matters in our lives. Our loving Heavenly Father sent Jesus to abide with us, live a sinless life, and die on the cross bearing our sins. When Jesus was victoriously raised from the grave, He made a way for us to move from death to life. Jesus wants to weed these sinful issues from our lives so we can be even more fruitful for Him and His Kingdom. This is the hard work of being a Christ-follower. (pg. 153)

Prayer

My Redeemer and My Salvation, thank You for the grace, mercy, and forgiveness You lavished on a flawed man like me. Thank You for completing in me that which I cannot do. Work in me to grow to become like You in the areas of anger, fear, lust, depression, and inconsistency. Move in me so that I may become even more fruitful for Your Kingdom. In my Savior's name. Amen.

Memory Verse

Let us not lose heart in doing good, for in due time we will reap if we do not grow weary. (Galatians 6:9)

SESSION 8

Growing in Fruitfulness

1. Now that you have gone through the previous seven sessions, name three to five principles you learned which will help you grow as a Christian man.

a.

b.

c.

d.

e.

2. Spend a few minutes honestly answering these diagnostic questions and then discuss them one-on-one with another person in your group. Place a mark where you fall on the spectrum found beneath each question.

How much did anger play a part of your life this last week?

◆--◆

Very little   A whole lot

How often did fear impact your life this last week?

◆--◆

Not at all   All the time

How often did lust hinder your spiritual walk this last week?

◆--◆

Rarely   Constantly

How often did you experience a spiritual funk this last week?

◆--◆

Never   A lot of the time

How consistent was your walk with Jesus this last week?

◆---◆

Wishy-washy   Rock solid

Did you spend time in prayer this last week?

◆---◆

Very little   Every day

Did you spend time in God's Word this last week?

◆---◆

Very little   Every day

What has your work/rest balance been this last week?

◆---◆

All work   All rest

Were you able to attend worship services this last week?

Yes   No

Have you connected with another Christian man this last week?

Yes   No

3. Why are questions like these important for Christian men to answer and to talk about with each other?

4. Do you have anyone you respect and can be honest with who can ask you these questions on a regular basis? If not, take a moment to pray and think about someone who might be able to fulfill this role in your life?

5. Now that you have completed the *Flawed to Fruitful* study, who do you know that you could take through this study on a one-on-one basis?

6. Would you be willing to pray for and seek out that man in order to disciple him, using this material?

Hope for Men

It has been my experience that in the darkest times of my ministry, our loving Father has granted me opportunities to serve other ministers. There have been times when I have questioned my effectiveness, and it is right at those times when a fellow pastor calls and needs to talk. Immediately, I forget my struggles and doubts, and run to listen to my brother. As I listen to him share his heart, my heart beats along with his and is freshly set afire with the call of God on my life. (pg. 109)

Prayer

My Great Teacher and Father, I ask now that You use me in the life of another man. Place someone in my life and in my heart who needs another man to guide him into spiritual maturity. Stir in me the desire to be that man in my friend's life. Work in both of us to become more and more like You. I ask this in the name of Jesus, the King of Kings and Lord of Lords. Amen.

Memory Verse

The things which you have heard from me in the presence of many witnesses, entrust these to faithful men who will be able to teach others also. (2 Timothy 2:2)

ABOUT THE AUTHOR

Rolland Kenneson has been in ministry leadership for over 30 years, serving churches and educational ministries throughout Colorado. He currently serves as pastor at Rosemont Baptist Church in Montrose, Colorado. His main mission in life is helping people find their identity in Christ igniting a passion within them to serve uniquely in the Body of Christ. Rolland received his bachelor's degree from Colorado Christian University and obtained his Master's degree from Southwestern Baptist Theological Seminary. He has been married to Rhonda since 1992. Together they have one daughter, Jessica, who works as a biochemist. When he is not pastoring, coaching, or ministering, Rolland loves spending time with his wife, woodworking, leatherworking, tinkering in the shop, fishing, and enjoying the beauty of Colorado.

SHELTERING TREE

EARTH PUBLISHING

Books, audios, videos, and podcasts
to help you feed His sheep.

ShelteringTreeMedia.com

Made in the USA
Columbia, SC
02 February 2025

53129518R00040